D0719091

impressions

A calligraphic journey through the wisdom of words

JIM BILLINGSLEY

ISBN 0 947338 68 3

This edition published 1996 exclusively for Selecta Book Ltd,
Folly Road, Roundway, Devizes, Wiltshire, UK.

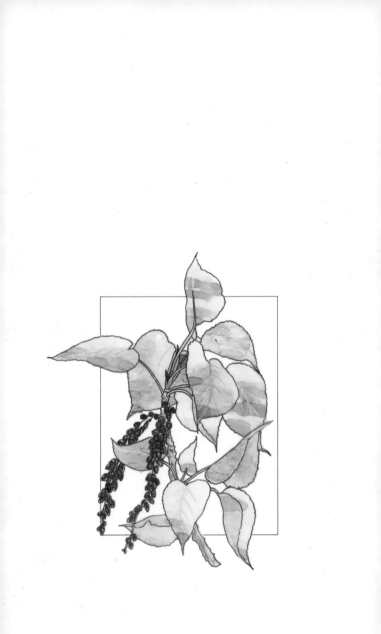

Look to this day!
For it is life, the very life of life.
In its brief course lie all the varieties
and realities of your existence;
The bliss of growth:
The glory of action:
The splendour of beauty:
For yesterday is always a dream,
and tomorrow is only a vision
But today, well lived makes every
                              yesterday
A dream of happiness, and every
                              tomorrow
a vision of hope.

Look well, therefore, this day!

To laugh often and much,
To win the respect of intelligent people
And the affection of children,
To earn the appreciation of honest critics
And endure the betrayal of false friends,
To appreciate beauty,
To find the best in others,
To leave the world a bit better,
Whether by a healthy child, a garden patch
Or a redeemed social condition,
To know even one life has breathed easier
Because you lived,

This is to have succeeded.

I love not Man the less,

But Nature more.

There is a pleasure
          in the pathless woods,

There is a rapture on the lonely shore,
There is society, where none intrudes,
By the deep sea, and music in its roar.

I love not Man the less,

But Nature more.

Byron

*Mix a little foolishness
with serious plans,
it's lovely to be silly
at the right moment.*

I shall not pass this way again
Through this toilsome world, alas!
Once and only once I show,
If a good deed I may do
To a suffering fellow man
No delay, for it is plain
I shall not pass this way again.

Character
is like a tree
And reputation like its shadow.
The shadow is what we think of it;

The tree is the real thing.

If there be righteousness in the heart,
There will be beauty in the character,
If there is beauty in the character,
There will be harmony in the home,
If there is harmony in the home,
There will be order in the nation,
Where there is order in the nation,
There will be peace in the world.

Lao Tse

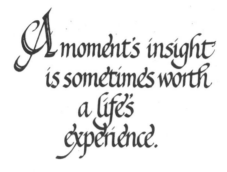

A moment's insight
is sometimes worth
a life's
experience.

Oliver Wendell Holmes

W

e choose

how we shall live;
courageously or in cowardice,
honourably or dishonourably,
with purpose or in drift.

We decide what is important
and what is trivial in life.

We decide what makes us significant
is either what we do or refuse to do...

We decide.
We choose

and as we decide and as we choose,
so our lives are formed.

THERE IS A TIME
FOR EVERYTHING
AND A SEASON
FOR EVERY ACTIVITY
UNDER HEAVEN

a time to be born and a time to die,
a time to plant and a time to uproot
a time to kill and a time to heal,
a time to tear down and a time to build,
a time to weep and a time to laugh,
a time to mourn and a time to dance,
a time to scatter stones and a time to gather them,
a time to embrace and a time to refrain,
a time to search and a time to give up,
a time to keep and a time to throw away?
a time to tear and a time to mend,
a time to be silent and a time to speak,
a time to love and a time to hate,
a time for war and a time for peace.

Ecclesiastes 3:1.8

ope
is the mechanism
that keeps
the human race
tenaciously alive,
dreaming,
planning,
building.

Hope is not the
opposite of realism...

It is the opposite
of cynicism
and despair

When we stop worrying
about troubles we have
and offer thanks for the
troubles we don't have,

happiness comes.

If you have built
castles in the air,
your work need not be lost;
there is where they should be.
Now put foundations under
them.

Henry David Thoreau

Change is a process,
not
an
event.

To the generous mind
the heaviest debt
is that of gratitude,
when it is not
in our power
to repay it.

The day
the child realises
that all adults are
imperfect, he becomes
an adolescent.
The day he forgives
them he becomes an
adult.
The day he forgives
himself
he becomes wise.

good nature

is the foundation of all virtues,
either religious or civil; good nature,
which is friendship between man and
man, good breeding in courts, charity
in religion and the true spring of all
beneficence in general.
Good nature and good sense must
ever join;

To err is human, to forgive, divine.
Good sense and good nature, by which
I mean beneficence and candour, is
the product of right reason, which
of necessity will give allowance
to the failing of others, by considering
that there is nothing perfect
in mankind.

Enlightened

The enlightened care
more about living
than winning

_I_ am indeed a practical dreamer...
I want to convert my dreams into
realities as far as possible.

Mahandas Gandhi

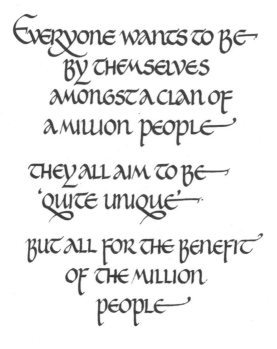

Everyone wants to be
by themselves
amongst a clan of
a million people

They all aim to be
'quite unique'

But all for the benefit
of the million
people

If I had my life to live over again,
    I'd try to make more mistakes next
    time.
I would relax; I would limber up; I
    would be sillier than I have been
    on this trip.
I know of very few things I would
    take seriously.
I would take more trips. I would be
    crazier.

I would climb more mountains, swim
    more rivers, and watch more
    sunsets.
I would do more walking and looking.
I would eat more icecream and less
    beans.
I would have more real troubles and
    fewer imaginery ones.

You see, I'm one of those people who live life prophylactically and sensibly hour after hour, day after day. Oh, I've had my moments, and if I had to do it over again, I'd try to have nothing else, just moments, one after another, instead of living so many years ahead of each day.

I've been one of those people who
never go anywhere without a
thermometer, a hot-water bottle,
a gargle, a raincoat, aspirin and
a parachute.
If I had to do it over again I would
go places, do things and travel
lighter than I have.

If I had my life to live over I would
start barefooted earlier in the
spring and stay later in the fall.
I would play hookey more.
I wouldn't make such good grades,
except by accident.
I would ride on merry-go-rounds,

I'd pick more
daisies..

Nadine Stair (aged 85 years)

When a person forgives another,
he is promising to do three things
about the intending wrong doing;
- not to use it against the wrong
  doer in the future;
- not to talk about it to others;
- and not dwell on it himself.

Learn from the mistakes
of others

You can't live long enough
to make them all
yourself.

Life is a ticklish
business;
I have resolved to
spend it in
reflecting
upon it.

Arthur Schopenhauer

One day at a time
this is enough.
Do not look back
and grieve over
the past
for it is gone...
And do not be troubled
about the future,
for it has not yet come.
Live in the present,
and make it so beautiful
that it will be worth
remembering.

If a child lives with hostility,
        he learns to fight.
If a child lives with criticism,
        he learns to condemn.
If a child lives with fear,
        he learns to be apprehensive.
If a child lives with jealousy,
        he learns to hate.
If a child lives with self-pity,
        he learns to be sorry for himself.
If a child lives with encouragement,
        he learns self-confidence and integrity.
If a child lives with praise,
        he learns to be appreciative.
If a child lives with acceptance,
        he learns to love.
If a child lives with approval,
        he learns to like himself.
If a child lives with fairness,
        he learns justice.
If a child lives with honesty,
        he learns what truth is.
If a child lives with friendliness,
        he learns that the world is a
        good place in which to live.

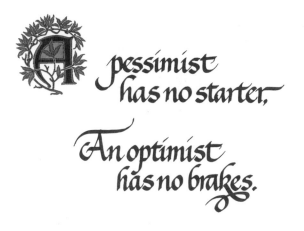

A pessimist
has no starter,

An optimist
has no brakes.

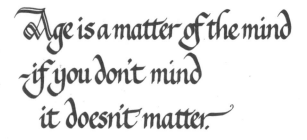

Age is a matter of the mind
-if you don't mind
it doesn't matter.

Men go forth to wonder
at the height of mountains,
the huge waves of the sea,
the broad flow of the ocean,
the course of the stars;
and forget to wonder
at themselves.

Augustine

Ambition

raises a secret tumult in the soul,
it inflames the mind, and puts it into
a violent hurry of thought: it is still
reaching after an imaginary good;
that has not in it the power to abate
or satisfy it.

Be not too fond of honour, wealth or
fame, since non of these can beautify
the mind; But may ambition and
your pride proclaim, and render you
the test of human-kind: When true
humility, without all these may make
you happy, and shall make you pleased.

*We sometimes from dreams
pick up some hint worth
improving by-reflection.*

Thomas Jefferson

Believe in yourself
It isn't always easy
Go slowly, enjoy the view

Take time to heal the pain
Rebuild yourself gently
Enhance your awareness
Knowledge is the key

Learn to soar
so you can be free

Sue Thomas

as I grow old

as I grow old it seems that I
grow old as grows the western sky
when day is coming to its close:
for life takes on a tint of rose
I had not known in life's hot noon.
now in the night that comes so soon
I see new stars I had not seen,
a surer faith, a peace serene,
as I grow old.

as I grow old the winds of life
die down, the hate, the hurt, the strife.
the waters calm, the waves are still,
I want no triumph, wish no ill
to any man. now from my heart
the ancient angers all depart.
new friends I know, new songs are sung,
new joys are mine ~
yes, I grow young
as I grow old!

Douglas Malloch